Etudes of Love

*Wisdom of the Inner Voice
Volume I*

Also by Sharon Lyn Shepard:

Etudes of Love
Wisdom of the Inner Voice, Volume I

Realizing our Divinity
Wisdom of the Inner Voice, Volume II

Labyrinth of Enlightenment
Wisdom of the Inner Voice, Volume III

Embodied Transformation
Wisdom of the Inner Voice, Volume IV

Consummating our Sovereignty
Wisdom of the Inner Voice, Volume V

Masters of Creation
Wisdom of the Inner Voice, Volume VI

Lighting the Way
Wisdom of the Inner Voice, Volume VII

Etudes of Love

Wisdom of the Inner Voice
Volume I

Sharon Lyn Shepard

Copyright © 2019 by Sharon Lyn Shepard

All rights reserved. This book or any portion thereof may not be reproduced or used in any manner whatsoever without the express written permission of the author except for the use of brief quotations with due credit to the author and link to the source. Thank you for respecting the words of this author.

The author of this book does not dispense medical or psychological advice or recommend the use of any specific technique or treatment without the advice of a physician or mental health professional. The information contained herein is only the author's personal experiences. In the event you use the information contained in this book for yourself, the author does not assume responsibility for your actions or outcomes.

"Wisdom of the Inner Voice" is a trademark of Sharon Lyn Shepard, All rights reserved.

ISBN: 9781087049229
www.sharonlynshepard.com

Foreword
by Sofia Peacock

So many words spring to mind in describing the poetry of Sharon Lyn Shepard. Inspirational, affirming, playful, light-filled, evocative, delightful, magical, comforting, profound and wise. And then, there are also no words . . . for etudes in deed they are! Her words are received by my heart as music - exquisite music - playing for the edification of my soul.

Like the poet herself, the poems are multi-dimensional and speak on many levels. Indeed a guidebook full of ancient wisdom, Sharon's poetry is also as a journal of her own spiritual journey and I sense the delicious daring with which she has walked her path. I feel that these writings are a manifestation birthed by the deepest desires of her heart, and also from ours.

This is one of those magical books where one can randomly open to a page and find the perfect message for that moment, filling the heart with wonder and appreciation. These messages feel so deeply personal and so sweet in that they remind me of what I know and then open me to "more".

I feel the power of her words, consciously chosen and woven with magical threads of Light. They activate, assist, and affirm. With great precision and clarity, these poems offer great support as they take us beyond the confines of duality and into empowered sovereign living.

Above all, I feel that Sharon sets the records straight about what Love really is.

This is a book of our times, for our times!

~ Sofia Peacock ~

The Etudes of Love
sing through me
as the primordial essence
that summoned me
into existence
flowing through my body
ever reminding me
of the original pulse of Love
the heartbeat of my GodSelf
and the eternal song of my Soul.

Prologue

Although I have spent much of my life with a pen in hand, I never set out to write poetry. Over the years, journaling has always been a way of articulating and grounding my life experiences. These journals have held a multitude of conversations between my human self, who was frequently floundering, and my soul who is always available with the necessary wisdom to take the next step forward, no matter how illogical it may sometimes seem. These conversations have always my been my soul food and the divine nectar for which my heart hungers as well as the guidance through my unforeseen ever-expanding spiritual journey.

One morning I awoke spontaneously writing poetry. When I pondered the change in my writing style I realized as I expand my consciousness my words need more space.... lots of space.... because each word is so expansive I need to pause and be fully present with each of them. Their energy began carrying a rhythm and a song of their own, free of the typical human chatter. These are the songs of my Soul, the distilled wisdom from all my daily experiences. They take me deep into the essence of Who I AM and bring a smile to my everyday activities of life.

This "Wisdom of the Inner Voice" is present within each of us. It whispers to you as your sacred and intimate lover. For it is the I AM, the one who has loved you into being, from your origin, through every lifetime, every experience, and every nuance of life for the simple passion of being. Your soul distills the essence of each of your experiences into pure wisdom, free of judgment, free of timelines, and free of your human conceived stories. It whispers from the depth of the silence offering divine guidance for the remembrance of who you are and have yet to become.

Humanity is in the midst of a renaissance of awakening, self-discovery, healing, and transformation. This cataclysmic shift is expanding our consciousness and awakening the realization of the totality of who we are as multidimensional beings creating a whole new paradigm in which to grow and thrive.

It has become my practice to listen to the Wisdom of the Inner Voice and record these words in the form of poetry. My inner sanctuary is a place of rich wisdom that can be called upon to ease the challenges of my daily life. It's also a place that fosters joyful expansion. Bridging my inner world with my outer world has become a passionate playground for my muse as our world is in the process of recreating itself. My desire to share this playground with others continues to be the impetus for my writing.

It is my joy and honor to share these words as a reflection of my experiences with anyone who is yearning for more ease and grace through this unprecedented transformation during our soul journey of remembering ourselves as embodied Divine Humans. It is my passion to inspire you to see the love and beauty within you to experience life with an open heart in touch with the magic bubbling up from within. My Beloveds, we have so much to celebrate together as humanity is awakening to a more enlightened consciousness as creators of a beautiful new world with infinite potentials and new avenues of joy. I invite you to allow the resonance of these words to sink into your heart to evoke and enliven your own Inner Voice of Wisdom with the inspiration to illuminate your own soul's path.

How To Best Enjoy this Book of Poetry

"Wisdom of the Inner Voice" is a series of poetry books that are best experienced in sequence to enhance your inner journey of Self discovery. Although each book stands alone, reading them sequentially will expand your consciousness by building upon your personal experiences of the prior volumes.

There are several ways to enjoy this poetry. Perhaps the first time, you'd like to read it through from beginning to end as a sacred inner journey. Or, you may prefer to read a poem a day for your meditative practice allowing it to take you deeper into your heart, savoring each word as if spoken from your own sacred lover. If you're in need of a particular passage, for example: love, compassion, clarity, courage, joy, or freedom, I invite you to visit "Wisdom of the Inner Voice" on my website where you will find accompanying artwork with each poem and a category list for your searching ease. My all time favorite way of using this book is to spontaneously open to a page and see what passage awaits. I invite you to revisit this book often for the words have a way of transforming themselves with each re-reading as we continue to journey together in our ever-expanding consciousness.

Contents

Call for Love — 19

- THE CALL FOR LOVE — 21
- YEARNING FOR LOVE — 23
- THE WAY OF LOVE — 25
- SWEET SURRENDER — 27
- THAT DEEP PLACE WITHIN — 29
- FOOTSTEPS OF LOVE — 31
- OPENING TO MORE — 33
- UNFILTERED LOVE — 35
- BEAUTY AND THE BEAST — 37
- MANY SPLENDORED BEING — 39
- LOVE YOUR HUMANNESS — 41
- COMMITMENT TO LOVE — 43

Divine Love — 45

- ETUDES OF LOVE — 47
- I AM THE SOURCE OF LOVE — 49
- ETERNITY OF LOVE — 51
- I AM LOVE — 53
- LANGUAGE OF LOVE — 55
- TRUST THE SOUL — 57
- FREELY FLOWING LOVE — 59

THE WAY OF DIVINE LOVE	61
THE ABYSS OF LOVE	63
INVITATION TO DIVINE LOVE	65
JOY OF DIVINE LOVE	67

Power of Love — 69

ROSE OF SHARON	71
SONG OF LOVE	73
I AM THE RIVER OF LOVE	75
YOUR PRESENCE OF LOVE	77
CHALICE OF LOVE	79
OVERFLOWING HEART	81
MIRACLES OF LOVE	83
POWER OF LOVE	85
FEAR OF LOVE	87
WELLSPRING	89
OF DIVINE LOVE	89
ELIXIRS OF DIVINE LOVE	91
LOVE IS WHO I AM	93

Surrender — 95

ALCHEMY OF LOVE	97
GIFT OF SURRENDER	99
THE PRODIGAL RETURNS	101
DIVINE KNOWING	103

THERE IS ONLY LOVE	105
BEAUTY OF SURRENDER	107
SWEET GENTLE CLEANSING	109
SOFT SURRENDER	111
SURRENDER TO THE DIVINE	113
BEGIN ANEW	115

Self Love   *117*

SACRED PATH OF SELF LOVE	119
THROUGH THE EYES OF GODSELF	121
LOVE OF THE HUMAN SELF	123
IT ALL CIRCLES BACK TO LOVE	125
IN SEARCH OF LOVE	127
ANNOYANCE	129
LOVE IS ALL INCLUSIVE	131
ATTACHMENT	133
RETURN TO LOVE	135
LOVE OF SELF	137
UNREQUITED LOVE	139

The Beloved   *141*

THE SEARCH IS OVER	143
BELOVED EMBODIMENT OF GOD	145
LOVE, HONOR, AND CHERISH	147
WHISPERS OF YOUR GODSELF	149

PRECIOUS HUMAN	151
LOVE YOUR HUMANNESS	153

Relationship — 155

IN SEARCH OF LOVE	157
SACRED LOVER	159
SMITTEN	161
SACRED RELATIONSHIP WITH SELF	163
TRUE RELATIONSHIP	165
LOVE INCARNATE	167
RELATIONSHIP WITH SELF	169
IN THE PRESENT MOMENT	171

Compassion — 173

COURAGE TO LOVE	175
THE ERUPTING HEART	177
FORGIVENESS	179
TIME OF SOFTENING	181
THE COMPASSION OF LOVE	183
FEEDOM OF FORGIVENESS	185
CONCEALED COMPASSION	187
COMPASSION OF THE SOUL	189
TRUE COMPASSION	191
AN INVITATION FROM THE HEART	193

Prelude

There is a sacred song that has continually drawn me deeper and deeper into my search for love. It is the ultimate love song, the song of my soul. Although it continues to be unwavering, it has often felt elusive and unrecognized by my human self.

"Etudes of Love" is a collection of poems written as Love songs between the soul and the human. They are the intimate songs of our soul calling us into the depths of our heart to commune with our true Beloved. They invite us into our sacred boudoir where the soul sings the wisdom of our inner voice beguiling the harmonic union of the human and the soul with the realization that we are the embodiment of Divine Love.

They are the revelations of the magnificence of Divine Love, a love pure and free of any judgment. A love that flows without the need to control or mitigate. A love that's at the core of who we are as our GodSelf, as the amalgamation of God and human.

As human beings we have a deep yearning for love. We treat love as a commodity, similar to how we treat money. We work at accumulating it and storing it in our hearts, much like a bank account. We only dole it out to those we feel deserving of our love. In turn, we are only able to fully accept love when we feel worthy of it, which is even less often. We look to spouses or friends to fill us with love, when in reality we are the love for which we have always been searching.

Humans have little, if any, experience with Divine Love. Once we remember the totality of who we are as Divine Humans, we realize we are Divine Love and always have been. This is the true relationship we have been seeking all of our lives.

May these words be a Love song to lure the opening of your heart. May they wrap themselves around you like a warm soothing blanket allowing you to feel safe enough to fully open your heart to experience Love in a way you have never experienced it before as the Love of the Divine.

This is where the journey of Self Realization begins, with the Love of self and the embodiment of our GodSelf. This is the soul food and the divine nectar for which the heart hungers offering guidance through our ever-expanding spiritual journey.

By surrendering to the alchemy of Love, fear is transformed into trust, doubt into wisdom, tears into grace, judgment into compassion, and chaos into harmony. The more your heart opens, the more Love will flow from within you until you become the over-flowing chalice of Divine Love enriching your life and all others.

I invite you to be still and quiet, allowing these sacred words to take you deep into your heart to remember the Love of who you are as a Divine Human, as your GodSelf in physical form.

Call for Love

THE CALL FOR LOVE

Do you hear the call
the call of your human self
calling out for more Love?

You hear it
in the pain or illness of your body.

You hear it
in your fear of not being loved by another.

You hear it
in your angst about the world events.

You hear it
in your anger at not being heard.

You hear it
in the sadness of loss.

Sometimes the call
is a soft whisper barely noticeable.

Other times it's roaring like a lion
rampant thoughts repeating in your head
a stab in the stomach
tears streaming down your face.

These are the calls
asking for self Love
easily remedied when you gently
wrap your arms around your human self
whisper, I Love You
and remember the truth of Who You Are
as the embodiment of Divine Love.

YEARNING FOR LOVE

The human yearns for love
searching here
searching there
for the love
that will heal
their deep seated wounds
that continue to hold love at bay.

The human yearns for love
searching here
searching there
for a love
that will fill
all the empty places within
that have been sorely abandoned.

The human yearns for love
often finding
a temporary love
a superficial facsimile of love
a love that blazes forth

then fizzles into ashes
when asked for too much in return.

The human
will never find true love
until it surrenders
its human expectations
and dives deeply within
where the embers
of Divine Love
are always present
asking nothing in return.

THE WAY OF LOVE

On days like this I need you near me
On days like this I need your help
I ask for courage, I ask for strength
I ask you to walk beside me hand in hand

Amidst my angst I need a friend
Amidst my turmoil I need peace
Chaos surrounds me, I've lost my way
I ask you to walk beside me hand in hand

In times like these I need a partner
In times like this I need support
My vision is clouded, I need clarity
I ask you to walk beside me hand in hand

To show me the way of love, the way of trust
the way of acceptance with compassion
Show me the way of grace
Show me the way

With you beside me my view expands

With you beside me I see what's real
I sink into my heart
and always live from Love

When you walk beside me hand in hand
I know the way of love, I live in trust
I live in acceptance with compassion
I know the way of grace
I know the way.

When you walk beside me hand in hand
I know the way of Love
I know Love.

~ Lyrics for the harp by Sharon Lyn Shepard ~

SWEET SURRENDER

Someone's calling from your heart
with a voice that's soft and sweet
filled with love songs from your Soul
ever calling, calling from your heart.

Love light's burning, shining from your heart
an eternal flame clear and bright
it's time to open fully to your soul
in sweet surrender, surrender to your heart.

Passion's flowing from deep within
streaming out in rivers of Love
Can you surrender to your heart?
Can you surrender, surrender to Joy?

Can you surrender to your heart
sweet surrender to your heart
sweet, sweet, sweet surrender.

~ Lyrics for the harp by Sharon Lyn Shepard ~

THAT DEEP PLACE WITHIN

Get in touch with that deep place within
that place that's been
neglected due to distractions
that place that's been
abandoned in response to others
that place that's been
restless with desire
that place that's been
calling out for your attention.

Get in touch with that deep place within
that place that's
overflowing with Love
that place that's
brimming with Creativity
that place that's
shimmering with Magic
that place that's
bubbling with Joy.
Get in touch with that deep place within
and continue to feed it.

FOOTSTEPS OF LOVE

Unconditional Love
seems like a monumental feat
requiring the sacrifice of the ego
offering the totality of one's self
at the foot of the altar.

No wonder the gates
to unconditional love
have not been flung wide open
by masses of humans
rushing to gain entrance
in hopes of attaining
this spiritual badge of the heart.

And yet. . .
'tis such an easy path taken one step at a time.

Simple acts of kindness
listening with an open heart
offering a hand where needed
smiling without a reason to smile

giving up the need to be right
honoring each other's path without judgment

These are all simple tasks
each of us can engage in
these are the footsteps
of Unconditional Love
that leave a trail behind us
amidst the bleakness
of a world that's gone asunder.

This is Unconditional Love, pure and simple.

OPENING TO MORE

The more Loving I am
the more open I become

The more Compassionate I am
the more peaceful I become

The more Grateful I am
the more abundance flows to me

Be Loving
Be Compassionate
Be Grateful

UNFILTERED LOVE

What if you could
love every one
and every thing?

Without the need
to filter your love?

BEAUTY AND THE BEAST

Beauty and the Beast
is not a faerie tale
it is the tale of the healing
of duality within each of us.

Beauty and the beast live side by side
the beast enticing her to love him
by bestowing upon her all the "things"
most women would desire.

But things do not entice her
it is the beauty of life
that makes her heart sing
as she lives side by side with the beast.

In the end,
it is the simplicity of her Love
that breaks the spell
and the beast is transformed.

This is the duality

that we are living right now
beauty living side by side
with the beast of darkness.

Do not judge the beast
for the beast has been bewitched
by the enchantment
of our material world.

In the end,
it is the simplicity of our Love
that will break the spell
and the beast of darkness
shall be transformed.

Be the Love that does not judge
Be the Love that transforms
Be the Love that is creating
a whole new world.

Be Love.

MANY SPLENDORED BEING

Love is a many splendored thing,
but your mind does not always believe that
for it has been dealing with the fickleness
of human love for so long
it has forgotten Divine Love
nor does it trust Divine Love.

Your mind is also a many splendored thing
for it has guided you
through many human lifetimes
to bring you safely to this point of transition
not to leave the body to realize your Divinity
but to fully embody your Divinity.

It's time to embrace the human mind
to fully Love it
as your sacred partner
to soothe its ruffled feathers
assure it of its sacred presence in your life
and invite it into the sanctuary of your heart.

As a Divine Human
you are the amalgamation
of the body, mind, and spirit,
an enlightened embodiment of the Divine
and an ever expanding consciousness
of All That Is.

Love is a many splendored thing
your Mind is a many splendored thing
your Divinity is a many splendored thing
and together...
YOU are a many splendored Being.

LOVE YOUR HUMANNESS

We are birthing a new world!
There is no need to fight the hypocrisy.
Allow the old to reveal itself for what it is
a broken system immeshed in the fear of loss.

Allow it to die peacefully
surrounded by our love.

For is that not what is happening
within each of us?
The death of the old
and the birthing of the new.

Love humanity
Love your humanness
Love where we have come from
and love the new.

COMMITMENT TO LOVE

Commitment to Love
is a moment-to-moment practice
until all those moments string together
and Love becomes our natural way of being.

Divine Love

ETUDES OF LOVE

The Etudes of Love
sing through me
the primordial essence
that summoned me
into existence
flowing through my body
ever reminding me
of the original pulse of Love
the heartbeat of my GodSelf
and the eternal song of my Soul.

I AM THE SOURCE OF LOVE

I AM the Love
that my human self
has been searching for.

I AM the source of the Love
that my human self
has been longing to trust.

'Tis only the judgment
perpetrated by my human mind
that stimulates my own lack of self Love
and stands in the way of the remembrance
of the Divinity of who I AM.

I AM Divine
I AM the source of Love
I AM Divine Love.

ETERNITY OF LOVE

I etch the words
I AM LOVE
into the grains
of glistening sand
where the tide
has gone out
with sea gulls
soaring overhead
and nary a human
has walked.

Throughout the day
I feel the essence
of this Love
absorbed into the sea
as the tide rushes in
spreading across
the distant shores
and my heart
busts forth
with passion.

There are those
who may think
that Love
is transient
but my heart knows
that Love
is eternal
continually spread
across distant shores
increasing my
own heart's passion.

I AM LOVE

Human love
with all its limitations
requires an exchange of love
I give you love
and consequently
I expect your love in return.

Whereas,
Divine Love radiates
from within my heart
ever present, ever expanding
without any need for
measurement, exchange,
nor possession.

I AM Divine Love
therefore. . .
I have no need to receive love
I have no need to give love
because
I AM already Love.

You are Divine Love
therefore...
there is no need to receive love
there is no need to give love
because
You are already Love.

When I know myself as Love
and
you know yourself as Love
we can Love freely
as Sovereign Beings
in Love with All That Is.

LANGUAGE OF LOVE

Words are not enough
for the language of love
words will never be enough
for the infinite presence of Love.

Words can never be enough
until Love speaks through our hearts
warm and kind, filled with compassion
with its gentle embrace.

Words can never be enough
until Love speaks through our joy
Love's splendor knows no bounds
bursting forth with delight.

Words can never be enough
until Love speaks through our soul
Love's wisdom flows pure and simple
guiding us with grace.

Words can never be enough

until Love speaks through our breath
the breath of life, breath of creation
breath of all-that-is.

Words can never be enough
until we dip into the well of Love
flowing with passion
flowing with beauty
flowing with infinite bliss.

Words are not enough for the Divinity of Love
Words can never be enough
because the infinite Presence of Love simply is
Love simply is.

~ Lyrics for the harp by Sharon Lyn Shepard ~

TRUST THE SOUL

The soul knows Love
in a way the human does not
the soul is always full
whereas the human in never satiated
constantly hungry for more.

You are in a human body
to realize and embody Divine Love
to perceive the sultry intimacies
and to savor all the flavors
that only Divine Love can provide.

As the human continues
to expand in Divine Love
there will always be
new playgrounds and
infinite opportunities to explore.

The soul will never lead you astray
at times it will take you by the hand
and lead you into the fray

intent on teaching you
to more fully open your heart
and accept everything that presents itself
as an opportunity to Love.

Trust the soul
Trust Love.

FREELY FLOWING LOVE

Do not allow your human love
to stand in the way
of your Divine Love.

Whereas human love
is riddled with
needless agendas.

Divine Love is
free flowing
with infinite purity.

THE WAY OF DIVINE LOVE

When I disengage
from the drama
of conversations
happening all around me
and quietly remain aligned
within my clear heart-space,
conversations shift
to Love and Kindness.

There is no effort on my part
it's simply the way of Divine Love.

THE ABYSS OF LOVE

Having walked away
from a world
that no longer feeds me

I Am
effortlessly
floating
in the Abyss of Love
with a heart wide open
to create anew.

INVITATION TO DIVINE LOVE

Invite Divine Love
to flow through you
washing away
all that is not of Love
filling those spaces
with Divine Love
to soothe and heal.

Invite Divine Love
to empower
All of Who You Are
as the Creator
of a new reality
to be fully lived
in Joy and Playfulness.

JOY OF DIVINE LOVE

Allow Divine Love
to effortlessly
carry you
moment
by
moment
into
ever expanding
experiences
of a joyful
fulfilling
life.

Power of Love

ROSE OF SHARON

Petals unfurl in the shimmering mist
in velvet folds, soft and rich
droplets of dew shine like pearls
on you, the rose of Sharon.

Your fragrance fills the air so sweet
wafting across hills and vales
in the rapture of morning's light
you, the rose of Sharon.

It hasn't always been this way
a life of velvet and sweet perfume
many a blossom failed to open
as the rose of Sharon.

Thorns appear where never planned
at the time it may bring tears
but in the end tears turn to dew
crowning the rose of Sharon.

Now your petals unfurl in the sun

dancing in the sway of the breeze
sweet and sensual, fragrant and free
you, the rose of Sharon.

You're the rose of Sharon
a beautiful rose of Sharon
Love embodied, radiant light
a beautiful, beautiful rose.

Love embodied, radiant light
a beautiful, beautiful rose.
a beautiful rose of Sharon.

~ Lyrics for the harp by Sharon Lyn Shepard ~

Note: Rose of Sharon means ...
"Consumed by Love" or "The Beloved One",
often referred to in "Song of Songs" in the bible.

SONG OF LOVE

At the heart of it all
there is a song
called Love

'Tis in the heart of man
and nature alike

'Tis in the heart
of every inanimate object

For where there is form
there is Love

And there is nothing
without the song of Love

I AM THE RIVER OF LOVE

I AM the River of Love
drawing you deeper
deeper into your body
deeper into your heart.

I AM the River of Love
bubbling over
the protective rocks
you've so carefully placed.

I AM the River of Love
dissolving your old beliefs
wearing them away
as easily as sand.

I AM the River of Love
flowing through you
transforming every cell in your body
to your Divinity.

I AM the River of Love

the guiding current
through the twists and turns of life
with infinite grace.

I AM the River of Love,
allow me to flow through you
returning you to your Divinity.

YOUR PRESENCE OF LOVE

You entered the world on a beam of light
radiant being filled with wonder
You danced in on a song of Love
bringing joy and delight.

You came in with a message of hope
a wealth of wisdom and compassion
You ushered in a time of harmony
with hope of a better world
a world of peace.

Your gift of presence, simple and pure
expands and grows, touching all.
Your hope and wisdom, love and joy,
awaken us to a world
of pure delight.

You touched our hearts
and they're bursting open
with your presence Love now grows
You fill our hearts to overflowing

with your presence Love now grows.

With your presence, Love grows.

~ Lyrics for the harp by Sharon Lyn Shepard ~
(dedicated to my beloved daughter, Lisa)

CHALICE OF LOVE

I offer love to you
from the chalice of the heart
doesn't matter who you are
man or woman, rich or poor
black or white, young or old
I offer this chalice of love to you.

My heart spills over
with the joy of life
and fills the chalice
with wine so rich
join me in sipping
from this cup
getting drunk
on the ecstasies of love.

It's the great mystery
how love heals all
but it's true
I tell you now
with a drop of love

wounds can mend
with understanding
wars can end.

Accept this gift
graciously given
there's no payment
this cup is free
all that I ask of you
is to receive it
and when you're ready
please pass it on.

Pass this cup of sweet, sweet wine
from your hand to another
as we all drink from
this chalice of love
One people, One heart.

~ Lyrics for the harp by Sharon Lyn Shepard ~

OVERFLOWING HEART

When you allow your heart
to be so full it's overflowing
Love, in all of its forms,
will be the mainstay of your Life.

MIRACLES OF LOVE

Step out of your worrisome life
beyond the deception of your human mind
into the wisdom of your heart
embracing all that Love imparts.

Live your life in the stream of creation
in abundance, infinite and free
partnering with Spirit in every moment
exploring the wonders and spender of life.

Live and create from the power of your truth
residing within the mystery of your heart
turn all your dreams into gold
in the cauldron of love, peace and joy.

Divine Love is the substance of miracles
expressing through you and me
stir your heart's cauldron of miracles
and watch how easily love abounds.

Miracles, all these miracles

miracles surround us
miracles of Life.

Miracles, all these miracles
Miracles of Love abound.

~ Lyrics for the harp by Sharon Lyn Shepard ~

POWER OF LOVE

I asked to be shown my gifts
to be shown where my power lies.

And with my request
the answer became very clear
My gift is Love
My power is Love.

I stand here, heart wide open
knowing I Am Love.

FEAR OF LOVE

There are many who say
I want love
I want to be loved
simultaneously fearing love
afraid to open their hearts
afraid of what love will do to them
afraid of what love will expect of them.

Love expects nothing.

However,
Love will change you
it will change how you see yourself
how you see and react to others
how you see and react to the world.

Love will consume you
Love will heal your broken heart
opening you to the infinite flow of pure Love
a Love that flows without bounds
a Love without expectations

a Love with glorious potentials
the Love of all that Is.

WELLSPRING OF DIVINE LOVE

An eternal wellspring of Divine Love
flows through your body
constantly feeding
nurturing and
rejuvenating your cells.

There is no need to suffer
no need to diminish
no need for dis-ease
those are human concepts
created by the mind.

Expanding
thriving
and evolving
and are at the root
of our Divine blueprint.

For we are all

omnipotent
omnipresent
omniscient
beings of the Universe.

Allow your mind to be filled
with the wellspring of Divine Love
overflowing to each and every cell.

Therein lies your healing
thriving, and joy.

ELIXIRS OF DIVINE LOVE

As you close your eyes
at the end of the day
take a deep breath
allowing the elixirs of Divine Love
to wash over you
through you
clearing your thoughts
easing your resistance
healing your body.

Before you open your eyes
in the morn
take a deep breath
allowing the elixirs of Divine Love
to fill you
overflowing
permeating every cell
of your body and mind
to initiate perfect well-being.

Whenever anything

or anyone triggers
your resistance
take a deep breath
allowing the elixirs of Divine Love
to dissolve the discord and
expand your consciousness
to the perfection
of All That Is.

The essence of Life
has never eluded us
the essence of Life
is ever flowing as Divine Love
drink of it with your breath
your heart and your mind.

Drink freely
and live the infinite fullness of Life.

LOVE IS WHO I AM

Beaming . . . Glowing. . . Loving
this is what my heart is always doing

I glow because Love is Who I Am.

Although life's circumstances
may not always feel aglow
my heart continues to glow
eternally, effortlessly
beaming Love.

During those times
when life feels asunder
I surrender to my heart
trusting that my heart
will never lead me astray

Take a moment and breathe this in
fully realizing your heart's glow
fully realizing the Love that You Are.

I Love because Love is Who I Am.

Surrender

ALCHEMY OF LOVE

By surrendering
to the alchemy of Love
fear is transformed into trust
doubt into wisdom
tears into grace
judgment into compassion
and chaos into harmony.

GIFT OF SURRENDER

With every expansion of consciousness
we awaken to a new level of knowing
which requires the surrendering
of what we thought to be true.

Surrender can be as easy
as taking a breath
or
surrender can become
a battle ground for the ego.

Whereas the ego thinks
surrender is loosing the battle
a giving up of what it thinks
is right and important

The evolved human knows
surrender is the divine grace
that dissolves all barriers
between us and our divine birthright.

Surrender
is a breath away
your expanded consciousness
is a breath away
your divine birthright
is a breath away.

THE PRODIGAL RETURNS

Your Soul has been patiently waiting
until you are ready to surrender your human self
into its arms, to embrace you
like the prodigal's son or daughter
who has returned to be enfolded in Love

You have done nothing wrong
there is nothing to forgive
you have simply been experiencing
the fullness of life as a human being
which is what you came here to do

Why vilify your past
working so hard at picking apart your life
to release your perceived mistakes
when these are the experiences
that have enriched your coffers

Is it not easier to recognize
the perfection of all of life
how each and every experience

has added to who you are
not taken away from who you are

At long last it is time
to allow your Soul to enfold
the essence of all your experiences
to proliferate the knowing of Self Love
and expand your Consciousness.

DIVINE KNOWING

I am not here to define life
I am here to experience life
for the joy of life itself
and to create with life.

The rightness or wrongness
of how we or anyone else
chooses to perceive life
is an old concept of duality.

When I surrender
my human need to know
Divine knowing shows itself
and expands upon itself.

When I surrender
my human need to know
I open to All That Is
allowing love and joy
to express through me
in childlike wonderment

and eternal excitement
to co-create with life!

THERE IS ONLY LOVE

The canyon that looms before you
causes your mind to tremble
afraid to take the leap.

But the closer you approach
the sooner you realize
it is the canyon of Divine Love.

You have feared the abyss
feared the unknown
afraid to take the leap.

Fear not Beloved
for by taking the leap
there are only two results.

One is to land on the other side
with your feet firmly
on the ground of Divine Love.

The other is to drop into the abyss

and be fully absorbed
into the Presence of Divine Love.

Thus I ask you,
why not take the Leap
because. . .
there is only Love.

BEAUTY OF SURRENDER

Surrender is a beautiful thing
to dive deeply
surrendering to oceans of Love.

And yet, the human mind resists
thinking it will loose control
and it does.

When the mind finally surrenders
what it finds beyond the confines of control
is peace, love, and joy.

When the human self finally surrenders
it realizes it has lost nothing
and gained everything.

SWEET GENTLE CLEANSING

Sweet gentle cleansing
as the heart opens more fully
crystalline tear drops
flow down our faces
allowing us
to see Love
in all its forms
to hear Love
whisper in the breeze
to feel Love
in the depth of our being

Allow the tears
for they are
the sweet elixirs of Love.

SOFT SURRENDER

I awoke enveloped in softness
a peaceful gentle softness
taking me deeper into the core of my Beingness
without the need to rush into the day.

I awoke enveloped in softness
relaxed and fluid
free of the angst of the world
without any need for protection or barriers.

Funny how we think of soft and gentle
as weak and cowardice
when in reality, with softness
I feel no need to be brave and strong.

Instead I feel a strength in being soft and gentle
for it is rooted in Love and Peace
at the sweet sweet center of the feminine
in soft surrender to the Power of my Divine.

SURRENDER TO THE DIVINE

What if…
instead of focusing on
the never-ending process
of attempting to let go
of all that the mind
continues to conjure.

What if...
you bow at the altar
of your heart
and
surrender it all
to the Divine.

BEGIN ANEW

I surrender
everything
to my GodSelf
and begin anew.

I surrender
to Love
and begin anew.

I surrender
to Peace
and begin anew.

I surrender
to Joy
and begin anew.

I surrender
and
begin anew.

Self Love

SACRED PATH OF SELF LOVE

The sacred path of self Love
is not one we've been taught
in fact we've been taught
the very opposite
that self love is selfish
narcissistic and egocentric.

But the overflowing truth is . . .
Love is the very core of who we are.

How can we love another
without knowing the truth of Love
the purity of Love
the wholeness of Love
the Divinity of Love?

That, Beloveds
is self Love.

If you do not Love your self
you know not who you are

and you have nothing
to offer another.

THROUGH THE EYES OF GODSELF

Your GodSelf does not degrade you.
and yet, you degrade your self
and you degrade others

When you see
through the eyes
of your GodSelf
life presents itself
with pure perfection
for you are the perfection of the Divine
bursting forth
in the eternal unfoldment of Love.

LOVE OF THE HUMAN SELF

We have been taught to love others
but the one who has suffered the most
is my human self
for all the judgment I have laid upon her
all the while giving myself away.

Today….
I am in tears with heart felt Love
for my human self
who never ceases to amaze me
with the resiliency of Love

No matter what I face
there is always Love.

IT ALL CIRCLES BACK TO LOVE

It all circles back to self Love
because in the eyes of the Divine
you are always worthy of Love.

No matter what appears to be broken
no matter what pains your heart
no matter what disrupts your peace
there is always something deeper
there is always Divine Love.

IN SEARCH OF LOVE

Our lurking shadows are our wounded parts
"acting out" in search of Love.

Those shadows are a sacred part of us
isn't it time to invite them into our heart space
to be nurtured with love and compassion
just like an innocent wounded child.

When we do, they revel in our love
and blossom into full radiant color
rather than continuing to "act out"
as the shadows of black and white.

ANNOYANCE

When someone annoys you
it's your annoyance with yourself
for they are simply reflecting
a place within you
that's out of alignment
with your GodSelf.

When you Love yourself
as your GodSelf . . .

Voila!! The annoyance dissolves
with ease and grace
and you're flying high.

LOVE IS ALL INCLUSIVE

Love is all inclusive
acting as the bridge between
the perceived good or bad.

No matter what obstacles arise
for yourself or others
the answer is always Love, Self Love.

Simply Love your Self
more and
more and
more.....

For it is your expanded Love of Self
that continues to expand All-That-Is
in perfect well-being and Divine alliance.

ATTACHMENT

Attachment to people
things or experiences
is an attempt to
fill a void within you
where there is
a lack of love.

How much easier
life becomes once you
realize the Love
innately within you
and allow everything
to come and go at pleasure.

RETURN TO LOVE

My emotional reactions
are always about me
never the other person

Thus as I stumble across things
that cause an adverse reaction
I go within

I disengage from the other person
I disengage from all the stories
and I return to Love

It really is that simple
I Love, Love, Love
until I am comfortable again

This Loving is not directed
at the other person or event
it is directed at my human self

I would not have experienced

an adverse reaction if I were
consciously aware of my self
as a body of Love

Once I return to Love
I am free
not of the situation
not of the person
but free from
my emotional reactions
that are rooted in my lack of self Love

My emotional freedom
always lies
in my return to Love.

LOVE OF SELF

Love of Self
knows no bounds.
It flows
like water
to all the open spaces
awaiting its soft caress.

Love of Self
is a sacred gift
to me
to you
and all that surrounds us.

Allow it to flow with ease and grace.

UNREQUITED LOVE

When past events cycle back around
vying for our attention
it's not about the person
it's not about the circumstances
it's not about who did what to whom
it's always about self Love.

Every instance of unrequited love
or judgment from another
left you feeling unloveable
eroding your own self love
leaving unloved pieces of your self
scattered throughout your unconscious.

Once the light shines upon them
vying for your attention
it's not the people or events
that need your attention
'tis the pieces of your self
that got left behind.

Go beyond the stories
gathering the pieces
into your heart space
with complete acceptance
embracing them
with boundless Divine Love.

Celebrate their homecoming
and recognize your Self
as whole and perfect
once again.

The Beloved

THE SEARCH IS OVER

The time for searching is over
for that which you
have been searching
is your Self.

Your Beloved,
the one who knows you
better than anyone else
the one who has the answers
to your every question
the one who will always
support your deepest desires
the one who has loved you
since before you were born.

Seek no longer
for you know all
that you will ever need to know
and you have all you will ever need
in the loving arms of your own BeLoved Self.

BELOVED EMBODIMENT OF GOD

Your physical body
is capable of embodying
the fullness of Who-You-Are.
The only thing that limits you
is your belief
of not being worthy

Being human is not a weakness
it is the ultimate
most intimate
way of experiencing life
as the Beloved
embodiment of God
in physical form

Do you not realize
that all beings
throughout the universe
are in awe of you

as a Divine Human
who walks this earth

Being in physical form
is the ultimate gift of Love

Treasure your humanness
Treasure your Divinity
Treasure the totality of Who-You-Are.

LOVE, HONOR, AND CHERISH

Love yourself
for you are the Divine in physical form.

Honor yourself
for having the courage to step into human form.

Cherish yourself
for you are the Beloved.

With Self Love
you take the reigns back into your own hands
because you'll never be in search of love again.

WHISPERS OF YOUR GODSELF

I love you
your GodSelf whispers.
But I just screwed up again
your human self answers.

It doesn't matter,
I love you
your GodSelf whispers.
But I'm not worthy
your human self answers.

I doesn't matter,
I love you
your GodSelf whispers.
But I know I can do better
your human self answers.

It doesn't matter,
I love you

your GodSelf whispers
and I will continue to tell you so
until you're able to love yourself
the way I do.

And then my Beloved,
you will realize
that you are God incarnate
and you will whisper
"I love you"
to everyone you meet
because you see them
as I see you.

PRECIOUS HUMAN

My beloved human
do you not realize
how precious you are?

You think your self
unworthy

You think your self
a sinner

You think your self
weak and ailing

You think your self
lacking

You think your self
unloveable

All these things
you think

with your mind

When you go
beyond the mind
beyond thinking

What you will find is
the perfection of
a cherished human

A precious human
that embodies all the divinity
of love, joy, and compassion.

There is nothing
more precious than
being human.

LOVE YOUR HUMANNESS

I Love you
says your GodSelf

I love your body
for it is the illustrious temple that houses me

I love your mind
for it is it allows you to grow in understanding

I love your spirit
for it is gives credence to your expanded consciousness.

I love your humanness
for it expresses All-That-Is in a myriad of ways.

Without you I would be nothing.
Without your body, mind, spirit, and humanness
you would be nothing.

Love your body

Love your mind
Love your spirit
Love your humanness
Rejoice in the Being you have become
and the Being that continues to expand
because of your Love.

Relationship

IN SEARCH OF LOVE

How much of my life have I spent
vying for your love?
I changed my appearance
I changed my actions
I even changed how I felt
always unsure
if you loved me.

But how could you love me
when you didn't even know me
because I never knew myself
as I shape-shifted
like a crazy chameleon
in response to you
in response to the world around me.

I finally realized
your love was never the issue
for it was my love of self
I was in search of
and now that I know who I Am

it matters not
if you love me or not.

For I am deeply enthralled
in a joyful passionate love affair
with my Divine Self
who lives within me
who is always here for me
who has always known
all of Who I Am.

SACRED LOVER

I whisper to you
as your sacred
and intimate lover
for that is who I AM
the one
who has loved you
into being
from your origin
through every lifetime
every experience
every nuance of life
expanding
your consciousness
your wisdom
your ability to enjoy life
with eternally new potentials
for the simple passion of being.

SMITTEN

I awoke
smitten with the Love affair
that's blossoming with my Self.

Enamored by the Love
that's always present
ever flowing
never judging

Infatuated with the Joy
that bubbles up from within
for no reason
other than I exist

Enchanted by the Magic
that playfully
continues to awaken
new aspects of me

Besotted with the flow
of everyday life

as I allow it
to have its way with me

No longer caught up in the old adages
of a human style love affair
addled with requirements
and unrequited expectations

Back in the arms of the Divine
sweet gentle embraced and content
crazy mad in Love with my Self
smitten in the knowing of Who I Am.

SACRED RELATIONSHIP WITH SELF

The most important thing
you can ever do for yourself
is to initiate
a Sacred relationship with your self
including all the parts
you've judged, put asunder
or hidden from yourself
for they too desire your love.

Once you embrace
all of Who You Are
judgment fades away
because you realize
there is nothing to judge
for everything in life
is a self created
Soul experience.

TRUE RELATIONSHIP

There is no one
that will ever love you
with the ultimate passion
that you can love your self
There is no spouse or friend
that will fill you up
and make you complete

For you are the I AM
the one who has
loved you into being
from your origin
through every lifetime
every experience
and every nuance of life

This is the true relationship
you have been seeking
all of your life.

LOVE INCARNATE

Your Divine Self
has always loved you

As you open yourself
to allow that Love to trickle in
your human self
begins to fall in love
with your humanness

And thus . . .
you are in the throws
of a passionate love affair
with the realization that
you have always been
and always will be
Love incarnate.

RELATIONSHIP WITH SELF

When we are comfortable
in our relationship with our Self
we become open and comfortable
in relationship to everyone
and everything else in our lives
and the need to conform
to someone we are not
to please another
simply dissolves.

IN THE PRESENT MOMENT

By being in the present moment
I see you as you are are,
pure and simple
free of the past
no worries about the future.

By being in the present moment
you see me as I am
pure and simple
free of the past
no worries about the future.

Being in the present moment
allows love to flow freely
opens doors of compassion
and initiates intimacy.

Being in the present moment
breaks the old bondage
freeing our relationships,
all relationships

to BE fresh and newly born
in every moment.

Compassion

COURAGE TO LOVE

It takes far more courage
to love than it does to hate,
far more courage to have compassion
than to inflict harm,
far more courage to see the God in you
no matter what you think of me.

It takes far more courage
for me to step away
from engaging in verbal warfare
once my mind has armed itself
with its incessant words
of mass destruction.

It takes far more courage
to lay down my weapons
of judgment and criticism
and allow my heart to lead
because my heart
sees the God in you.

It takes courage to Love
and courage to embrace with Compassion.
How courageous can you be?

THE ERUPTING HEART

Everything is erupting!
Words are flying
energies are exploding
our feelings
our personal lives
and the world stage.

And yet, everything that's erupting
is all about Love.

At the core
it is the Heart that's erupting
no longer willing to be ignored
no longer willing to be walled in
no longer willing to be contained.

For some this feels like
long awaited freedom
for others
it's like pulling off the scab
of a festering wound.

Healing requires love and compassion

Can you be
the love and compassion
the world needs right now
as all that is not Love
is imploding upon itself

Can you be
the love and compassion
the world needs right now
until it results in free flowing
unadulterated Love for all.

FORGIVENESS

Forgiveness is
a Divine Gift of Grace
that opens our hearts to Love
with the innocence of a child
beyond blame or guilt
allowing everyone equal footing
to be right and true
to their own GodSelf.

TIME OF SOFTENING

This is a time of softening
softening the heart
to allow Love to flow
softening the mind
to connect with Divine Intelligence
softening the body
with the Breath of Life
softening our attitudes
with Compassion
softening our vision
to attain Clarity
softening our voices
with Gentleness
softening our actions
with Kindness
softening our way of BEing in the world
softening with the Divine flow of Grace.

THE COMPASSION OF LOVE

The compassion of Love
brings all that has been hidden in the darkness
everything that needs clearing and forgiveness
all to the surface with ease and grace.

There is no need to process all the dross
there is no need to figure it all out
simply open your heart
and allow Love to do what it does best.

As you move through this healing process
know that you are being rocked
in the sweet gentle bosom
of Love and Compassion.

FEEDOM OF FORGIVENESS

Forgiveness is the ultimate act of letting go
freeing ourselves from the endless cycles
of judgment, victim-hood,
blame, shame, and guilt.

Forgiveness isn't directed toward another
It's our own expectations,
not someone one else's
that set us up for the fall.

Therefore,
Forgiveness is a precious gift to one's self
because for-giving is the giving forth of Love.

Once we truly love ourselves
all judgment and blame dissolves
and compassion becomes our natural way of life.

CONCEALED COMPASSION

Call upon the Compassion
of the Mother.

Go deeply
deeply into it
and you will find
that it was always
your own Compassion
concealed by the heavy laden
experiences of your life.

Once exposed
by your desire to Love
your Compassion flows freely
as a welcome comfort to yourself
and all who encounter
your Divine presence.

COMPASSION OF THE SOUL

The deeper we go
within our selves
the more of our unconsciousness
is brought to the surface
playing out in full view.

As the dross is stirred,
the more raw
the more tender
the more vulnerable
we allow ourselves to be
with what feels threatening,
the more easily it's dissolved
by the light of day.

What is revealed
is the love and compassion
our soul has for us
with its all-knowing wisdom
ever guiding us
with the most gentle

ease and grace
when we allow.

Breathe deeply, Beloved
invite the revelations
of your soul
to introduce you
to the totality of
the Divine Love
that you are
with its gentle
ease and grace.

TRUE COMPASSION

Compassion
does not require me
to join you in your suffering.

Otherwise
there would be nothing
but suffering in this world.

Compassion is
our ability to see the passion
of love and joy and say
come, this is the way home.

AN INVITATION FROM THE HEART

Compassion
is an invitation from the heart
to dissolve our walls of protection
to awaken our passion for life.

Come Passion,
open my heart
allow the infinite Love within me
to flow without bounds.

Come Passion,
allow my love for humanity
to be free of judgment
and embrace all that is.

Come Passion,
my tender intimate lover
smother me with kisses of the Divine
that I may know myself as you do.

Come Passion,
open my heart
allow the infinite Love within me
to flow without bounds.

Thank You!

Thank you for joining me on this sacred journey of Self discovery. If you're reading the kindle version you may also enjoy having a paperback copy to keep by your bedside. If you've found solace or inspiration here, please share this book with your friends and take a moment to leave a brief review on the site where you purchased it. Your response will help other readers make good reading choices. Authors depend on word of mouth and reviews, but very few readers leave reviews so your opinion can make a real difference. May your kind generosity return to you multiplied many fold!

Sharon Lyn Shepard
Mystic ~ Writer ~ Musician

Sharon Lyn Shepard is a modern day mystic, visionary, dream weaver, melody maker, and maestro of words. Her prose and music open hearts, transcend minds, and expand our consciousness, awakening us to our innate Divinity to access our own soul's wisdom. Because she has a conscious foot in multiple worlds, she is adept at articulating and grounding the essence and transformations we are experiencing during our journey of Self-Realization.

After retiring from her professional career as a physical therapist, energetic healer, ordained minister, and spiritual coach, she spent seven years following her divine guidance as a bohemian world traveler. Through her multi-cultural experiences she has come to realize all the travails of life are opportunities to expand our consciousness amidst our Soul journey of self-Love and Self-remembrance to ignite the infinite magnificence lying dormant within each of us.

Sharon has learned to create her own reality as heaven on earth. Her mystic writings, books, and harp music transcend our minds, taking us to the deepest recesses of our hearts to dip into our passion and overflowing cauldron of miracles to celebrate life with love and joy. Her words are an invitation to expand our consciousness, embody our GodSelf, and celebrate the bounty of every precious moment.

After years of travel, Sharon has settled in the Pacific NW where she has made her home in the midst of a forest on an island in the Puget Sound. She spends her time writing, composing music on her harp, gardening, and playing with the faeries of the forest.

Visit Me On My Website

A Sacred Sanctuary of Rest, Repose, Wisdom, and Expanded Consciousness

I invite you to visit my website where I offer a Sacred Sanctuary free of the noise and distractions of daily life, a place of rest, repose, wisdom, and rejuvenation.

Here you will find "Wisdom of the Inner Voice" a treasure trove of my poetry with accompanying artwork and a category list for your searching ease, for example: love, compassion, clarity, courage, joy, or freedom. Enjoy my zest for life and exuberance for creation on my blog "Divine Musings". And initiate an intimate connection with the Black Madonna via the "Black Madonna Diaries".

May these offerings provide comfort in knowing you are not alone as we share this adventure of ever-expanding consciousness to create a new reality for our world. I encourage you to visit often and relax into its safe haven of serenity and nurturance as a touch stone for your enlightenment.

www.sharonlynshepard.com

Then hop over to my Amazon Author's page. Click the "Follow" button to be advised of newly released books and more!!

www.amazon.com/author/sharonlynshepard

More from Wisdom of the Inner Voice

Etudes of Love
Wisdom of the Inner Voice, Volume I

Realizing our Divinity
Wisdom of the Inner Voice, Volume II

Labyrinth of Enlightenment
Wisdom of the Inner Voice, Volume III

Embodied Transformation
Wisdom of the Inner Voice, Volume IV

Consummating our Sovereignty
Wisdom of the Inner Voice, Volume V

Masters of Creation
Wisdom of the Inner Voice, Volume VI

Lighting the Way
Wisdom of the Inner Voice, Volume VII

Embrace A New World

Companion CD

Harp and Vocals by Sharon Lyn Shepard
Gold Metal Winner of IPA Music Awards 2016
for Inspirational Category

I invite you to join me on a musical spiritual journey to relax into your heart free of time and space, soar on the wings of angels, dance with the stars, and listen to the whispers of your heart. Most of this music was composed in synchronicity with the poetry of "Wisdom of the Inner Voice."

Winds of Change
Embrace a New World
Passages
I Don't Always Know
Bring me Home
Whispers of the Heart
Power of the Night
On the Wings of Spirit
Dance with the Stars
Love Grows
I Celebrate Life

* Available for purchase at Amazon.com

CPSIA information can be obtained
at www.ICGtesting.com
Printed in the USA
LVHW041935100220
646416LV00002B/710